SHE SAID

SHE SAID

Witty Words from Wise Women

COMPILED BY
Dominique Enright

Michael O'Mara Books Limited

First published in paperback in 2023

This edition first published in Great Britain in 2018
First published in 2000 as *Witty, Wicked and Wise* by
Michael O'Mara Books Limited
9 Lion Yard
Tremadoc Road
London SW4 7NQ

A CIP catalogue record for this book is available
from the British Library.

This product is made of material from well-managed,
FSC®-certified forests and other controlled sources.
The manufacturing processes conform to the
environmental regulations of the country of origin.

ISBN: 978-1- 78929-540-5 in paperback print format
ISBN: 978-1-78929-387-6 in ebook format

1 2 3 4 5 6 7 8 9 10

Cover design by Ana Bjezancevic, using an
illustration from Shutterstock
Designed and typeset by Claire Cater
Printed and bound by CPI Group (UK) Ltd, Croydon, CR0 4YY

www.mombooks.com

INTRODUCTION

Sharp of tongue and sharp of wit – here is a fascinating selection of the best of women's quotations throughout history, collected from as early as 700 BC right up to the twenty-first century. There is something here to appeal to everyone, whether it is witty comments on politics and public figures, wicked remarks about friends and family, or wise words on life and love.

For those accustomed to standard dictionaries of quotations – where there are at least ten quotations from men to every one from a woman – it might come as a surprise that there are so many well-established and published women writers. How many people have heard of Hypatia, for example, the fourth-century Greek philosopher, writer, astronomer and mathematician? Or the tenth-century Japanese writers Sei Shōnagon and Murasaki Shikibu?

And if you think, well, this was a long time ago, think again. Few today will have come across the actress and playwright Susannah Centlivre (*c.* 1669–1723), who wrote nineteen plays and was admired by Alexander Pope. The eighteenth century spawned a great number of now rarely read women writers such as Marguerite Blessington, who wrote novels and a book about Byron and travelled extensively; Hannah Cowley, who wrote plays; and Hannah More, a member of the Blue Stocking Circle and a most energetic playwright.

The truth is that history is littered with prolific and praiseworthy women who have been cast into the shadows by 'worthier' men.

And what do women have to say about that? 'As for you men, you may, if you please, live and be slaves,' scorned Boudica. 'Even his ignorance is of a sounder quality,' pronounced George Eliot of men in general. 'Why don't you write books people can read?' complained James Joyce's wife, Nora, and Mrs Gladstone was certainly not afraid to tell her husband, the Prime Minister, that he could be pretty boring at times.

Of course, some women have stood up to men, history and time: Elizabeth I, Jane Austen, George Eliot, George Sand, Helen Keller, Dorothy Parker, Coco Chanel and Gertrude Stein, to name just a few. Whatever walk of life they hailed from, readers will delight in the pithy pronouncements of those included here, from the forthright Sarah Josepha Hale (1788–1879), who is credited with 'Mary Had a Little Lamb' and the creation of Thanksgiving as a US national holiday, to the splendidly acerbic Helen Rowland (1875–1950), to the precocious but sadly short-lived Marjory Fleming (1803–1811) who succumbed to measles.

The last word should always lie with a woman:

> 'We hold these truths to be self-evident,
> that all men and women are created equal.'
> *Elizabeth Cady Stanton (1815–1902)*

SOCIAL
CALLINGS

Civility costs nothing and buys everything.

Lady Mary Wortley Montagu (1689–1762)

Incessant company is as bad
as solitary confinement.

Virginia Woolf (1882–1941)

Superior people never make long visits.

Marianne Moore (1887–1972)

Minute attention to propriety stops
the growth of virtue.

Mary Wollstonecraft Godwin (1759–1797)

It is bad *ton* to overwhelm with insipid flattery all
women that we meet, without distinction of age, rank or
merit. It may indeed please some of light and frivolous
minds, but will disgust a woman of good sense.

Madame Celnart (1796–1865)

I do not want people to be
very agreeable as it saves
me the trouble of liking
them a great deal.

Jane Austen (1775–1817)

Tact is after all a kind of mind-reading.

Sarah Orne Jewett (1849–1909)

Nothing is so delicate as the reputation of
a woman; it is at once the most beautiful
and most brittle of all human things.

Jane Welsh Carlyle (1801–1866)

Good taste is the worst vice ever invented.

Edith Sitwell (1887–1964)

Until you've lost your reputation, you never realize
what a burden it was or what freedom really is.

Margaret Mitchell (1900–1949)

Manners are a sensitive awareness of the feelings
of others. If you have that awareness, you have
good manners, no matter what fork you use.

Emily Post (1873–1960)

MEALS
AND
MANNERS

The tragedy of English cooking is that 'plain' cooking cannot be entrusted to 'plain' cooks.

Marcelle Azra Hincks, Countess Morphy (c. 1874–1938)

The English never smash in a face. They merely refrain from asking it to dinner.

Margaret Halsey (1910–1997)

I rang for ice, but this is ridiculous.

Madeleine Talmage Astor (1893–1940) as she was being helped over the rail of the Titanic, April 1912

We invite people like that to tea, but we don't marry them.

Hester Alice Stapleton-Cotton, Lady Chetwode (1851–1930) on her son-in-law-to-be John Betjeman

Surely she had endured enough for one evening without having to listen to intelligent conversation?

Stella Gibbons (1902–1989)

There's nothing on earth to do here but look at the view and eat. You can imagine the result since I do not like to look at views.

Zelda Fitzgerald (1900–1948)

TALK AND TITTLE-TATTLE

There is no such thing as conversation. It is an illusion.
There are intersecting monologues, that is all.

Rebecca West (1892–1983)

Blessed is the man who, having nothing to say,
abstains from giving in words evidence of the fact.

George Eliot (Mary Ann Evans, 1819–1990)

Rumour never delays.

Hrotsvitha of Gandersheim (c. 935– c. 1000)

Have you heard of the terrible family They,
And the dreadful, venomous things They say?
Why, half of the gossip under the sun,
If you trace it back, you will find begun
In that wretched House of They.

Ella Wheeler Wilcox (1855–1919)

Report is mightily given to magnify.

Fanny Burney (Frances, Madame d'Arblay, 1752–1840)

I never speak behind people's backs. If I've anything nasty to say, I pop it on a postcard.

Victoria Wood (1953–2016)

Bette and I are very good friends. There's nothing I wouldn't say to her face – both of them.

Tallulah Bankhead (1902–1968) on Bette Davis

. . . in few people is discretion stronger than the desire to tell a good story.

Murasaki Shikibu (c. 973–c. 1031)

She tells enough white lies to ice a wedding cake.

Margot Asquith (Countess of Oxford and Asquith, 1864–1945) on Lady Desborough

If you do not tell the truth about yourself you cannot tell it about other people.

Virginia Woolf (1882–1941)

At a party in Hollywood:

Jean Harlow: Why, you are Margott Asquith, aren't you?

Lady Asquith: No, my dear. I am Margot Asquith. The 't' is silent, as in Harlow.

Nobody is such a fool as to moider away his time in the slipslop conversation of a pack of women.

Lady Hester Stanhope (1776–1839)

When anger spreads through the breast, guard thy tongue from barking idly.

Sappho (c. 630–c. 570 BC)

His very frankness is a falsity. In fact, it seems falser than his insincerity.

Katherine Mansfield (1888–1923) on her husband John Middleton Murry

If it's very painful for you to criticize your friends – you're safe in doing it. But if you take the slightest pleasure in it – that's the time to hold your tongue.

Alice Duer Miller (1874–1942)

Nobody speaks the truth when there's
something they must have.
Elizabeth Bowen (1899–1973)

On every formal visit a child ought to be of the
party by way of provision for discourse.

Jane Austen (1775–1817)

I'll not listen to reason. Reason always means
what someone else has got to say.

Elizabeth Gaskell (1810–1865)

To-day I pronunced a word which should never come out
of a lady's lips it was that I called John a Impudent Bitch.

Marjory Fleming (1803–1811)

BEHIND CLOSED DOORS

It doesn't matter what you do in the bedroom as long as you don't do it in the street and frighten the horses.

Mrs Patrick Campbell (Beatrice Stella Tanner, 1865–1940)

~~~

If all the girls attending it were laid end to end . . . I wouldn't be at all surprised.

Dorothy Parker (1893–1967) referring to the Yale Prom, 1934, attr.

~~~

Wit in women is apt to have bad consequences; like a sword without a scabbard, it wounds the wearer and provokes assailants. I am sorry to say the generality of women who have excelled in wit have failed in chastity.

Elizabeth Montagu (1720–1800)

~~~

A man can sleep around, no questions asked, but if a woman makes nineteen or twenty mistakes she's a tramp.

Joan Rivers (1933–2014)

When a man seduces a woman, it should,
I think, be termed a left-handed marriage.

Mary Wollstonecraft Godwin (1759–1797)

Ducking for apples – change one letter
and it's the story of my life.

Dorothy Parker (1893–1967)

All my lovers have been geniuses; it's
the one thing on which I insist.

Isadora Duncan (1878–1927)

The worst sin – perhaps the only sin –
passion can commit, is to be joyless.

Dorothy L. Sayers (1893–1957)

Love ceases to be a pleasure when
it ceases to be a secret.

Aphra Behn (1640–1689)

There are no more thorough prudes than those who have some little secret to hide.

George Sand (Amandine-Aurore Lucille Dupin, Baronne Dudevant, 1804–1876)

~~~

Brevity is the soul of lingerie, as the Petticoat said to the Chemise.

Dorothy Parker (1893–1967), attr.

~~~

People are always asking me in interviews, 'What do you think of foreign affairs?' I just say, 'I've had a few.'

Dolly Parton (1946–)

~~~

Once I was with two men in one night. But I could never do it again – I could hardly walk afterward. Two dinners? That's a lot of food.

Sarah Silverman (1970–)

I have heard much of these languishing lovers,
but I never yet saw one of them die for love.

Margaret of Navarre (Marguerite d'Angoulême,
Queen of Navarre, 1492–1549)

~~~

I once went to one of those parties where
everyone throws their car keys into the middle
of the room. I don't know who got my moped
but I've been driving that Peugeot for years.

Victoria Wood (1953–2016)

~~~

It is well within the order of things
That man should listen when his mate sings;
But the true male never yet walked
Who liked to listen when his mate talked.

Anna Wickham (1884–1947)

~~~

I'll come and make love to you at five
o'clock. If I'm late, start without me.

Tallulah Bankhead (1902–1968)

MONEY

I must say, I hate money but it's the lack of it I hate most.

Katherine Mansfield (1888–1923)

\\\\\\\\\\\\\

Come away; poverty's catching.

Aphra Behn (1640–1689)

\\\\\\\\\\\\\

There are people who have money
and people who are rich.

Coco Chanel (Gabrielle Bonheur, 1883–1971)

\\\\\\\\\\\\\

People say that money is not the key to
happiness, but I always figured if you have
enough money, you can have a key made.

Joan Rivers (1933–2014)

\\\\\\\\\\\\\

Adversity is solitary, while prosperity dwells in a crowd.

Marguerite de Valois (1553–1615)

\\\\\\\\\\\\\

Prosperity seldom chooses the side of the virtuous.

Héloïse (1098–1164)

I have known many people who turned their gold into smoke, but you are the first to turn smoke into gold.

Queen Elizabeth I (1533–1603) to Sir Walter Raleigh

\\\\\\\\\\

It costs a lot of money to look this cheap!

Dolly Parton (1946–)

\\\\\\\\\\

Leave off the agony, leave off style,
Unless you've got money by you all the while

Julia A. Moore (1847–1920)

\\\\\\\\\\

. . . money demoralizes even the giver.

Marceline Desbordes-Valmore (1786–1859)

\\\\\\\\\\

Business is other people's money.

Delphine de Girardin (1804–1855)

\\\\\\\\\\

If we had no winter, the spring would not be so pleasant; if we did not sometimes taste of adversity, prosperity would not be so welcome.

Anne Bradstreet (1612–1672)

A Yankee (I speak of the common-minded) calculates his generosity and sympathy as methodically as his income; and to waste either, on an unprofitable, or undeserving, object would be foolish, if not wicked.

Sarah Josepha Hale (1788–1879)

. . . he had never heard Americans conversing without the word 'DOLLAR' being pronounced between them.

Frances Trollope (1780–1863)

A large income is the best recipe for happiness I ever heard of. It certainly may secure all the myrtle and turkey part of it.

Jane Austen (1775–1817)

Poverty? Wealth? Seek neither –
One causes swollen heads,
The other, swollen bellies.

Kassia (c. 810–c. 865)

I do want to get rich but I never want to
do what there is to do to get rich.

Gertrude Stein (1874–1946)

///////////

The longer I live, the more I grow in the
opinion that it is useless to pile up wealth.

*Françoise d'Aubigné, Madame de Maintenon
(1635–1719), governess to Louis XIV's children;
she married him after the queen's death*

///////////

Nothing melts a woman's heart like gold.

Susannah Centlivre (c. 1669–1723)

///////////

Money alone determines your entire
life, political as well as private.

Germaine Necker, Madame de Staël (1766–1817)

///////////

People don't resent having nothing
nearly as much as too little.

Ivy Compton-Burnett (1884–1969)

APPEARANCE

The perpetual hunger to be beautiful and that thirst to be loved which is the real curse of Eve.

Jean Rhys (1890–1979)

~

I, myself, am deeply superficial.

Fran Lebowitz (1950–)

~

Nature gives you the face you have at twenty; it is up to you to merit the face you have at fifty.

Coco Chanel (Gabrielle Bonheur, 1883–1971)

~

A high altar on the move.

Elizabeth Bowen (1899–1973) on Edith Sitwell's appearance

~

You look rather rash my dear your colors don't quite match your face.

Daisy Ashford (Margaret Devlin, 1881–1972)

~

Looking fifty is great – if you're sixty.

Joan Rivers (1933–2014)

A dirty exterior is a great enemy
to beauty of all descriptions.

Mary Martha Sherwood (1775–1851)

~~~

If you can't be better than your
competition, just dress better.

Anna Wintour (1949–)

~~~

Vanity, like murder, will out.

Hannah Cowley (1743–1809)

~~~

They always do [ask me to lose weight]. They want
to hire part of me, not all of me. They want to
hire about three-fourths, so I have to get rid of the
fourth somehow. The fourth can't be with me.

Carrie Fisher (1956–2016)

~~~

Her body has gone to her head.

Barbara Stanwyck (1907–1990) on a rising film star

As she had no hope of raising herself to the rank of a beauty, her only chance was bringing others down to her own level.

Emily Eden (1797–1869)

The sense of being well-dressed gives a feeling of inward tranquillity which religion is powerless to bestow.

Miss C. F. Forbes (1817–1911)

To write, to read, or think, or to enquire
Would cloud our beauty . . .

Anne Finch (1661–1720)

Happiness is in your power, though beauty is not; and on that to set too high a value would be pardonable only in a weak and frivolous mind.

Fanny Burney (Frances, Madame d'Arblay, 1752–1840)

Beauty endures for only as long as it can be seen; goodness, beautiful today, will remain so tomorrow.

Sappho (c. 630–c. 570 BC)

A lot of times girls think they're funny, but they want to be pretty at the same time, and if you want to be funny, you have to be willing to get ugly.

Amy Sedaris (1961–)

When a woman looks at a man in evening dress, she sometimes can't help wondering why he wants to blazon his ancestry to the world by wearing a coat with a long tail to it.

Helen Rowland (1875–1950)

If it were the fashion to go naked, the face would be hardly observed.

Lady Mary Wortley Montagu (1689–1762)

'Good heavens!' said he, 'if it be our clothes alone which fit us for society, how highly we should esteem those who make them.'

Marie von Ebner Eschenbach (1830–1916)

I'm not offended by all the dumb blonde jokes, because I know I'm not dumb . . . and I also know that I'm not blonde.

Dolly Parton (1946–)

Man is of a dull, earthy, and melancholy aspect, having fallowes in his face, and a very forrest upon his chin, when our soft and smooth cheeks are a true representation of a delectable garden of intermixed roses and lilies.

*Mary Tattlewell (*The Women's Sharp Revenge, *1640)*

It is now eleven years since I have seen my figure in a glass, and the last reflection I saw there was so disagreeable, that I resolved to spare myself the mortification in the future.

Lady Mary Wortley Montagu (1689–1762)

I would gladly give half of the wit with which I am credited for half of the beauty you possess.

Germaine Necker, Madame de Staël (1766–1817) to Juliette Récamier

I've had so much plastic surgery, when I die they will donate my body to Tupperware.

Joan Rivers (1933–2014)

You have to stay in shape. My grandmother, she started walking five miles a day when she was 60. She's 97 today and we don't know where the hell she is.

Ellen DeGeneres (1958–)

There were very few beauties, and such as there were were not very handsome ... Mrs Blount was the only one much admired. She appeared exactly as she did in September, with the same broad face, diamond bandeau, white shoes, pink husband, and fat neck.

Jane Austen (1775–1817)

Any girl can be glamorous. All you have to do is stand still and look stupid.

Hedy Lamarr (1914–2000)

To me Edith looks like something that would eat its young.

Dorothy Parker (1893–1967) on Dame Edith Evans

It is hardly surprising that women concentrate on the way they look instead of what is in their minds since not much has been put in their minds to begin with.

Mary Shelley (1797–1851)

Beauty with all the helps of Art, is of no long date; the more it is help'd, the sooner it decays.

Mary Astell (1666–1731)

A homely face and no figure have aided many women heavenward.

Minna Antrim (1861–1950)

That's the trouble, a sex symbol becomes a thing. But if I'm going to be a symbol of something, I'd rather it be sex than some of the things we've got symbols of . . . I just hate to be a thing.

Marilyn Monroe (1926–1962)

AGE

Exchange in a doorway:
Clare Boothe Luce, stepping aside: Age before beauty.
Dorothy Parker, sweeping through: Pearls before swine.

But the fruit that can fall without shaking
Indeed is too mellow for me.

Lady Mary Wortley Montagu (1689–1762)

Once I was looking through the kitchen window at dusk
and I saw an old woman looking in. Suddenly the light
changed and I realized that the old woman was myself. You
see, it all happens on the outside; inside one doesn't change.

Molly Keane (1904–1996)

The years that a woman subtracts from her age are not
lost. They are added to the ages of other women.

Diane de Poitiers (1499–1566)

We grow old as soon as we cease to love and trust.

Louise-Honoré de Choiseul (1734–1801)

We are always the same age inside.

Gertrude Stein (1874–1946)

One of the signs of passing youth is the birth
of a sense of fellowship with other human
beings as we take our place among them.

Virginia Woolf (1882–1941)

Please stop debating about whether or not I aged well.
Unfortunately, it hurts all three of my feelings.

Carrie Fisher (1956–2016)

One of the many things nobody ever tells you about middle
age is that it's such a nice change from being young.

Dorothy Canfield Fisher (1879–1958)

We grow neither better nor worse as we
get old, but more like ourselves.

May Lamberton Becker (1873–1958)

I refuse to admit that I am more than fifty-two, even if that does make my sons illegitimate.

Nancy, Lady Astor (1879–1964)

One keeps forgetting old age up
to the very brink of the grave.

(Sidonie-Gabrielle) Colette (1873–1954)

In youth we learn; in age we understand.

Marie von Ebner-Eschenbach (1830–1916)

Youth is the time of getting, middle age of
improving, and old age of spending.

Anne Bradstreet (1612–1672)

If youth is the season of hope, it is often so only in
the sense that our elders are hopeful about us.

George Eliot (Mary Ann Evans, 1819–1890)

A woman has the age she deserves.

Coco Chanel (Gabrielle Bonheur, 1883–1971)

When a noble life has prepared for old age, it is not decline that it reveals, but the first days of immortality.

Germaine Necker, Madame de Staël (1766–1817)

It is so comic to hear oneself called
old, even at ninety I suppose!

Alice James (1848–1892)

I'm not interested in age. People who tell me
their age are silly. You're as old as you feel.

Elizabeth Arden (1878–1966)

We grow old more through indolence,
than through age.

Christina, Queen of Sweden (1626–1689)

We are tomorrow's past.

Mary Webb (1881–1927)

You can stay young as long as you can learn,
acquire new habits and suffer contradiction.

Marie von Ebner Eschenbach (1830–1916)

Very young people are true
but not resounding instruments.

Elizabeth Bowen (1899–1973)

Eyes of youth have sharp sight, but commonly
not so deep as those of elder age.

Queen Elizabeth I (1533–1603)

Surely the consolation prize of age is in finding out how
few things are worth worrying over, and how many
things that we once desired, we don't want any more.

Dorothy Dix (1861–1951)

POLITICS

I have changed my ministers, but I have
not changed my measures. I am still for
moderation and will govern by it.

Queen Anne (1665–1714) to a new Tory ministry

Congress . . . these – for the most part – illiterate
hacks whose fancy vests are spotted with gravy and
whose speeches, hypocritical, unctuous and slovenly,
are spotted also with the gravy of political patronage.

Mary McCarthy (1912–1989)

Proud Prelate, you know what you were before
I made you what you are now. If you do not comply
with my request, I will unfrock you, by God.

Queen Elizabeth I (1533–1603) to Dr Richard Cox

The argument of the broken window pane is the
most valuable argument in modern politics.

Emmeline Pankhurst (1858–1928)

Once in a Cabinet we had to deal with the fact that there had been an outbreak of assaults on women at night. One minister suggested a curfew; women should stay home after dark. I said, 'But it's the men who are attacking the women. If there's to be a curfew, let the men stay home, not the women.'

Golda Meir (1898–1978)

From politics, it was an easy step to silence.

Jane Austen (1775–1817)

Political controversies are never entered into with any wish to gain knowledge, but only a triumph for the party.

Sarah Josepha Hale (1788–1879)

Never lose your temper with the Press or the public is a major rule of political life.

Christabel Pankhurst (1880–1958)

An election is coming.
Universal peace is declared,
and the foxes have a sincere
interest in prolonging the
lives of the poultry.

George Eliot (Mary Ann Evans, 1819–1890)

There is freedom of speech in Iran,
but there's no freedom after you've spoken.

Shappi Khorsandi (1973–)

~~~

Freedom is always and exclusively freedom
for the one who thinks differently.

Rosa Luxemburg (1871–1919)

~~~

O liberty! O liberty! What crimes
are committed in thy name.

*Jeanne-Marie, Madame Roland (1754–1793);
her last official words before being guillotined
for opposing Robespierre and Danton*

~~~

The most subversive thing a woman can do
is talk about her life as if it really matters.

Mona Eltahawy (1967–)

~~~

Morality must guide calculation, and
calculation must guide politics.

Germaine Necker, Madame de Staël (1766–1817)

A society in which consumption has to be artificially stimulated in order to keep production going is a society founded on trash and waste, and such a society is a house built on sand.

Dorothy L. Sayers (1893–1957)

If American politics are too dirty for women to take part in, there's something wrong with American politics.

Edna Ferber (1887–1968)

Political questions are far too serious to be left to the politicians.

Hannah Arendt (1906–1975)

I shall be an autocrat: that's my trade. And the good Lord will forgive me: that's his.

Catherine the Great, Empress of Russia (1729–1796)

. . . arbitrary power is, like most other things that are very hard, very liable to be broken.

Abigail Adams (1744–1888)

I don't agree with all-male leaderships. Men cannot be left to run things on their own. I think it's a thoroughly bad thing to have men-only leadership.

Harriet Harman (1950–)

I will make you shorter by the head.

Queen Elizabeth I (1533–1603) to the leaders of her Council when they opposed her policy on Mary, Queen of Scots

History is busy with us.

Marie-Antoinette, Queen Consort of France (1755–1793) at the revolutionary tribunal

Well, I've got you the presidency – what are you going to do with it?

Florence Harding (1860–1924) to her husband, US President Warren G. Harding

Well, Mr Baldwin, *this* is a pretty kettle of fish!

Queen Mary (1867–1953) to the Prime Minister, on the abdication of her son, Edward VIII

Authority without wisdom is like a heavy axe
without an edge, fitter to bruise than polish.

Anne Bradstreet (1612–1672)

Lying is an occupation
Used by all who mean to rise;
Politicians owe their station
But to well-concerted lies.

Laetitia Pilkington (1712–1750)

The pursuit of politics is religion,
morality, and poetry all in one.

Germaine Necker, Madame de Staël (1766–1817)

No influence so quickly converts a radical into
a reactionary as does his election to power.

Elisabeth Marbury (1856–1933)

But politics poison the mind.

Marceline Desbordes-Valmore (1786–1859)

POLITICIANS

He speaks to Me as if I was a public meeting.

Queen Victoria (1819–1901) on the British
Prime Minister William Gladstone

If you weren't such a great man you'd be a terrible bore.

Catherine Gladstone (1812–1900) to her
husband William Gladstone

. . . two-thirds mush and one-third [his wife] Eleanor.

Alice Roosevelt Longworth (1884–1980) on her distant
cousin, US President Franklin D. Roosevelt

A man you can bait with a tweet is not a man
we can trust with nuclear weapons.

Hillary Clinton (1947–) on US President Donald Trump

He has a brilliant mind until he makes it up.

Margot Asquith (Countess of Oxford and Asquith,
1864–1945) on Sir Stafford Cripps

He looks as if he had been weaned on a pickle.

Alice Roosevelt Longworth (1884–1980)
on US President Calvin Coolidge

How can they tell?

Dorothy Parker (1893–1967), on hearing that
US President Calvin Coolidge was dead

He's very clever, but sometimes his brains go to his head.

Margot Asquith (Countess of Oxford and
Asquith, 1864–1945) of F. E. Smith

He could not see a belt without hitting below it.

Margot Asquith (Countess of Oxford and Asquith,
1864–1945) on David Lloyd George

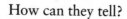

Thomas Dewey is just about the nastiest little
man I've ever known. He struts sitting down.

Lillian Dykstra, of the American politician Thomas E. Dewey

He would kill his own mother just so that he could use her skin to make a drum to beat his own praises.

Margot Asquith (Countess of Oxford and Asquith, 1864–1945) on Winston Churchill

WAR AND PEACE

That kind of patriotism which consists
in hating all other nations.

Elizabeth Gaskell (1810–1865)

Before a war military science seems a real science, like
astronomy; but after a war, it seems more like astrology.

Rebecca West (1892–1983)

The heresy of one age becomes the orthodoxy of the next.

Helen Keller (1880–1968)

Providence is always on the side of the big battalions.

Marie de Rabutin-Chantal, Madame de Sévigné (1626–1696)

Establishing lasting peace is the work of education;
all politics can do is keep us out of war.

Maria Montessori (1870–1952)

It is better to die on your feet
than to live on your knees.

Dolores Ibarruri, 'La Pasionaria' (1895–1989)

Mankind is not disposed to look narrowly into the conduct of great victors when their victory is on the right side.

George Eliot (Mary Ann Evans, 1819–1890)

△ ▲ △

They have not wanted peace at all; they have wanted to be spared war – as though the absence of war was the same as peace.

Dorothy Thompson (1894–1961)

△ ▲ △

Monarchs ought to put to death the authors and instigators of war, as their own enemies and as dangers to their states.

Queen Elizabeth I (1533–1603)

△ ▲ △

Every political good carried to the extreme must be productive of evil.

Mary Wollstonecraft Godwin (1759–1797)

△ ▲ △

I do not want the peace which passeth understanding, I want the understanding which bringeth peace.

Helen Keller (1880–1968)

We are not interested in the possibilities
of defeat; they do not exist.

Queen Victoria (1819–1901)

Kansas had better stop raising corn and begin raising hell.

Mary Elizabeth Lease (1850–1933)

Standing as I do, in view of God and eternity, I
realize that patriotism is not enough. I must have
no hatred or bitterness towards anyone.

*Edith Cavell (1865–1915), just before her execution
by the Germans on trumped-up charges of spying*

Pray, good people, be civil. I am the *Protestant* whore.

*Nell Gwynne (1650–1687), when, during the Popish Terror
of 1681, her coach was surrounded by an angry anti-
Catholic mob under the impression she was another of
Charles II's mistresses, Louise de Kéroualle, 'the Catholic
whore', whom the King made Duchess of Portsmouth*

People who talk about peace are very
often the most quarrelsome.

Nancy, Lady Astor (1879–1964)

PLACES

It is not in the temper of the people
either to give or to receive.

Frances Trollope (1780–1863) on the Americans

Canada is useful only to provide me with furs.

Jeanne Antoinette Poisson,
Madame de Pompadour (1721–1764)

What a pity, when Christopher Columbus
discovered America, that he ever mentioned it.

Margot Asquith (Countess of Oxford
and Asquith, 1864–1945)

The United States is . . . a warning rather
than an example to the world.

Lydia Maria Child (1802–1880)

America is my country and Paris is my home town.

Gertrude Stein (1874–1946)

In the United States there is more space where nobody is than where anybody is. That is what makes America what it is.

Gertrude Stein (1874–1946)

One has no great hopes from Birmingham.
I always say there is something direful in the sound.

Jane Austen (1775–1817)

New York . . . that unnatural city where everyone
is an exile, none more so than the American.

Charlotte Perkins Gilman (1860–1935)

There is small danger of being starved in our
land of plenty [America]; but the danger
of being stuffed is imminent.

Sarah Josepha Hale (1788–1879)

I am American bred.
I have seen much to hate here – much to forgive,
But in a world where England is finished and dead,
I do not wish to live.

Alice Duer Miller (1874–1942)

ARTS

So you're going to Australia! I made twenty
thousand pounds on my tour there, but of course
that will never be done again . . . All I can say is
– sing 'em muck! It's all they can understand!

Dame Nellie Melba (1861–1931)
to Dame Clara Butt

I would rather be a brilliant memory than a curiosity.

Emma Eames (1865–1982), opera singer,
on her early retirement at the age of forty-seven

If art does not enlarge men's sympathies,
it does nothing morally.

George Eliot (Mary Ann Evans, 1819–1890)

An unalterable and unquestioned law of the musical world
required that the German text of French operas sung by
Swedish artists should be translated into Italian for the
clearer understanding of English-speaking audiences.

Edith Wharton (1862–1937)

Music is not written in red, white and blue.
It is written in the heart's blood of the composer.

Dame Nellie Melba (1861–1931)

If I didn't start painting,
I would have raised chickens.

Grandma Moses (1860–1961)

Another unsettling element in modern art is
that common symptom of immaturity, the dread
of doing what has been done before.

Edith Wharton (1862–1937)

Señor Dalí, born delirious
Considers it folly to be serious.

Phyllis McGinley (1905–1978)

Oh, well, you play Bach *your* way. I'll play him his.

Wanda Landowska (1877–1959), attr.

There is less in this than meets the eye.

*Tallulah Bankhead (1902–1968), remark
to Alexander Woollcott on a performance of
Maeterlink's Aglavaine and Sélysette*

You ask my opinion about taking the young
Salzburg musician into your service. I do not know
where you can place him, since I feel you do not
require a composer, or other useless people.

*Maria Theresa, Empress of Austria (1717–1780),
to her son Archduke Ferdinand of Austria,
about the sixteen-year-old Mozart*

It's beige! My colour!

*Elsie DeWolfe (1865–1950)
on first seeing the Acropolis*

Of all the bulls that live, this hath the greatest ass's ears.

Queen Elizabeth I (1533–1603) on John Bull, musician and composer

Mrs Ballinger is one of those ladies who pursue Culture in bands, as though it were dangerous to meet it alone.

Edith Wharton (1862–1937)

Mr Lewis's pictures appeared to have been painted by a mailed fist in a cotton glove.

Edith Sitwell (1887–1964)
on Wyndham Lewis

Any man who has money may obtain the reputation of taste by the mere purchasing of the works of art.

Sarah Josepha Hale (1788–1879)

For painters, poets and builders have very high flights, but they must be kept down.

Sarah, Duchess of Marlborough (1660–1744)

WRITERS

No entertainment is so cheap as reading,
nor any pleasure so lasting.

Lady Mary Wortley Montagu (1689–1762)

One may lie to oneself, lie to the world, lie to
God even, but to one's pen one cannot lie.

Willa Cather (1873–1947)

I suppose I'm a born novelist,
for the things I imagine are more vital and
vivid to me than the things I remember.

Ellen Glasgow (1873–1945)

We again repeat that we will not accept any
stories where runaway horses or upsetting of
boats is necessary to the denouement.

Sarah Josepha Hale (1788–1879)

The great thing about writers who are not alive
is that you don't meet them at parties.

Fran Lebowitz (1950–)

Correct English is the slang of prigs who write
history and essays. And the strongest
slang of all is the slang of poets.

George Eliot (Mary Ann Evans, 1819–1890)

This is not a novel to be tossed aside lightly.
It should be thrown with great force.

Dorothy Parker (1893–1967) on Claudia Particella,
l'Amante del Cardinale *by Benito Mussolini, attr.*

It was a book to kill time for those who like it better dead.

Rose Macaulay (1889–1958)

Novelists should never allow themselves
to weary of the study of real life.

Charlotte Brontë (1816–1855)

If I read a book that impresses me,
I have to take myself firmly in hand before
I mix with other people; otherwise they
would think my mind rather queer.

Anne Frank (1929–1945)

All autobiographies are alibi-ographies.

Clare Boothe Luce (1903–1987)

A woman must have money and a room
of her own if she is to write fiction.

Virginia Woolf (1882–1941)

Satire should, like a polished razor keen,
Wound with a touch that's scarcely felt or seen.

Lady Mary Wortley Montagu (1689–1762)

But 'twill appear, in spite of all editing,
A woman's way to charm is not by writing.

Anne Finch (1661–1720)

Your poetry is bad enough, so pray
be sparing of your prose.

Elizabeth, Lady Holland (1771–1845)
to the poet Samuel Rogers

∿∿∿

Virginia Woolf's writing is no more than glamorous
knitting. I believe she must have a pattern somewhere.

Edith Sitwell (1887–1964)

∿∿∿

That old Yahoo George Moore . . .
His stories impressed me as being on the whole
like gruel spooned up off a dirty floor.

Jane Barlow (1860–1917)

∿∿∿

Very Tiresome Things: When a poem of one's
own, that one has allowed someone else to
use as his, is singled out for praise.

Sei Shōnagon (c. 966–c. 1025)

∿∿∿

The stupid person's idea of the clever person.

Elizabeth Bowen (1899–1973)
on Aldous Huxley

He seems to me the most vulgar-minded genius
that ever produced a great effect in literature.

George Eliot (Mary Ann Evans, 1819–1890)
on Lord Byron

∿∿∿

I am sorry to hear you are going to publish
a poem. Can't you suppress it?

Elizabeth, Lady Holland (1771–1845)
to Lord Porchester

∿∿∿

Besides Shakespeare and me,
who do you think there is?

Gertrude Stein (1874–1946)

∿∿∿

He gets at the substance of a book directly;
he tears out the heart of it.

Mary Knowles (1733–1807)
on Samuel Johnson

∿∿∿

Indeed, the freedom with which Dr Johnson
condemns whatever he disapproves is astonishing.

Jane Welsh Carlyle (1801–1866)

He and I should not in the least agree of course,
in our ideas of novels and heroines; – pictures of
perfection as you know make me sick and wicked.

Jane Austen (1775–1817) in a letter to her niece,
Fanny Knight, referring to Fanny's erstwhile
suitor, James Wildman. Fanny had lent him her
aunt's novels, which he did not like

∧∧∧

Then why didn't you bring him with you?
I should be delighted to meet him.

Emerald, Lady Cunard (Maud Alice Burke, 1872–
1948) to Somerset Maugham when he said he was
leaving some social occasion 'to keep his youth'

∧∧∧

The Doctor has a transcendental gift,
when he is writing sense, for making
this appear to be nonsense . . .

Edith Sitwell (1887–1964) of F. R. Leavis

∧∧∧

Oh, really? What is she reading?

Dame Edith Evans (1888–1876) when told that Nancy Mitford
had borrowed a friend's villa in order to finish a book

The affair between Margot Asquith
and Margot Asquith will live as one of the
prettiest love stories in all literature.

Dorothy Parker (1893–1967) on Margot
Asquith's four-volume autobiography

〰〰〰

What a sense of superiority it gives one to escape
reading some book which everyone else is reading.

Alice James (1848–1892) – perhaps thinking
of her brother Henry James's novels

〰〰〰

I wish her characters would talk a little less like
the heroes and heroines of police reports.

George Eliot (Mary Ann Evans, 1819–1890)
on Charlotte Brontë

〰〰〰

I don't care for Osbert's prose; the
rhododendrons grow to such a height in it.

Virginia Woolf (1882–1941) on Osbert Sitwell

Why don't you write books people can read?

Nora Joyce (1884–1965)
to her husband, James

A dirty man with opium-glazed eyes and rat-taily hair.

Lady Cavendish (Lucy Caroline Lyttelton,
1841–1925) on Alfred, Lord Tennyson

∿∿∿

The old maid among novelists.

Rebecca West (1892–1983) on H. G. Wells . . .
with whom she had a ten-year love affair

∿∿∿

His ignorance was an Empire State Building
of ignorance. You had to admire it for its size.

Dorothy Parker (1893–1967), on the editor
of the New Yorker, *Harold Ross*

∿∿∿

When you were a little boy, someone ought
to have said 'Hush' just once.

Mrs Patrick Campbell (Beatrice Stella Tanner,
1865–1940) to George Bernard Shaw

∿∿∿

Mamma says that she was then the prettiest, silliest, most
affected husband hunting butterfly she ever remembers.

Mary Russell Mitford (1787–1855)
on Jane Austen

I think I may boast myself to be, with all possible vanity, the most unlearned and uninformed female who ever dared be an authoress.

Jane Austen (1775–1817)

The carping malice of the vulgar world, who think it a proof of sense to dislike every thing that is writ by women.

Susannah Centlivre (c. 1669–1723)

Perpendicular, precise and taciturn.

Mary Russell Mitford (1787–1855) on Jane Austen

I would venture to guess that Anon, who wrote so many poems without signing them, was often a woman.

Virginia Woolf (1882–1941)

WOMEN

Women have been called queens for a long time,
but the kingdom given them isn't worth ruling.

Louisa May Alcott (1832–1888)

No woman is all sweetness; even the rose has thorns.

Juliette Récamier (Jeanne Françoise Julie Adélaide
Bernard, Madame de Récamier, 1777–1849)

A woman's tongue is a deadly weapon and the most
difficult thing in the world to keep in order, and things
slip off it with a facility nothing short of appalling.

Elizabeth von Arnim (1866–1941)

. . . women are the architects of society.

Harriet Beecher Stowe (1811–1896)

A woman's hopes are woven of sunbeams;
a shadow annihilates them.

George Eliot (Mary Ann Evans, 1819–1890)

I think if women would indulge more
freely in vituperation, they would enjoy
ten times the health they do.

Elizabeth Cady Stanton (1815–1902)

One must choose between loving
women and knowing them.

Ninon (Anne) de Lenclos (1620–1705)

It goes far towards reconciling me
to being a woman when I reflect I am thus
in no danger of marrying one.

Lady Mary Wortley Montagu (1689–1762)

The great and almost only comfort about being a
woman is that one can always pretend to be more
stupid than one is and no one is surprised.

Freya Stark (1893–1993)

But what is woman? – only one
of Nature's agreeable blunders.

Hannah Cowley (1743–1809)

She wants to be perfect. That is her defect . . .
It is vexatious that she is an angel. I
had rather she were a woman.

Marie-Anne, Marquise du Deffand (1697–
1780) on Madame de Choiseul

. . . spite will make a woman do more than love . . .

Margaret of Navarre (Marguerite d'Angoulême,
Queen of Navarre, 1492–1549)

Many women, who have little or no sense
of gratitude, have a very quick one of jealousy.

Eliza Haywood (c. 1693–1756)

Women are never stronger than when they
arm themselves with their weaknesses.

Marie-Anne, Marquise du Deffand (1697–1780)

Being a woman has only bothered me in climbing trees.

Frances Perkins (1882–1965); she was the first woman
to be a member of a US presidential cabinet

There is no female mind. The brain is not an organ of sex. As well speak of a female liver.

Charlotte Perkins Gilman (1860–1935)

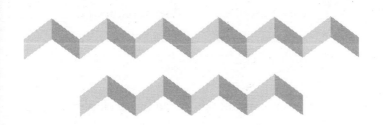

EQUALITY
FOR
WOMEN

How much it is to be regretted, that the
British ladies should ever sit down contented to
polish, when they are able to reform; to entertain,
when they might instruct; and to dazzle for an
hour, when they are candidates for eternity!

Hannah More (1745–1833)

I myself have never been able to find out precisely
what feminism is: I only know that people call
me a feminist whenever I express sentiments that
differentiate me from a doormat or a prostitute.

Rebecca West (1892–1983)

The Queen is most anxious to enlist every one who
can speak or write to join in checking this mad,
wicked folly of 'Women's Rights', with all its attendant
horrors, on which her poor feeble sex is bent, forgetting
every sense of womanly feeling and propriety.

*Queen Victoria (1819–1901) in a letter
to Sir Theodore Martin*

I do not wish them to have power over men; but over themselves.

Mary Wollstonecraft Godwin (1759–1797)

When a man gives his opinion he's a man. When a woman gives her opinion she's a bitch.

Bette Davis (1908–1989)

Woman, a pleasing but short-lived flower,
Too soft for business and too weak for power:
A wife in bondage, or neglected maid:
Despised if ugly; if she's fair, betrayed.

Mary Leapor (1722–1746)

The women who do the most work get the least money, and the women who have the most money do the least work.

Charlotte Perkins Gilman (1860–1935)

So long as women are slaves, men will be knaves.

Helen Rowland (1875–1950)

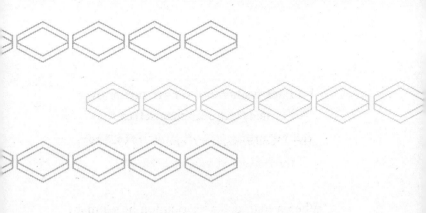

If women can be railroad workers in Russia, why can't they fly in space?

Valentina Tereshkova (1937–), the first woman in space

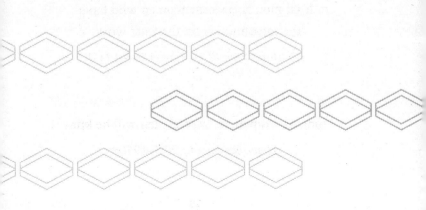

I ask no favours for my sex . . .
All I ask of our brethren is that they
will take their feet off from our necks.

Sarah Moore Grimké (1792–1873)

Woman's discontent increases in exact
proportion to her development.

Elizabeth Cady Stanton (1815–1902)

Is it to be understood that the principles
of the Declaration of Independence bear no
relation to half of the human race?

Harriet Martineau (1802–1876)

We hold these truths to be self-evident,
that all men and women are created equal.

Elizabeth Cady Stanton (1815–1902)

God would not give us the same talents if what
were right for men were wrong for women.

Sarah Orne Jewett (1849–1909)

I'd like to get to the point where I can
be just as mediocre as a man.

Juanita Kreps (1921–2010)

Men of sense in all ages abhor those customs
which treat us only as the vassals of your sex.

Abigail Adams (1744–1818)

If women want any rights they had better
take them and say nothing about it.

Harriet Beecher Stowe (1811–1896)

I was the first woman to burn my bra – it took
the fire department four days to put it out.

Dolly Parton (1946–)

Fireside occupation is one of the rights
of women that men may envy.

Hannah Farnham Lee (1780–1865)

I'm not surprised at what I've done.

Margaret Knight (1838–1914), an inventor, especially of heavy machinery, responding to the inevitable remarks

I truly believe that women should be financially independent from their men. And let's face it, money gives men the power to run the show. It gives men the power to define value. They define what's sexy. And men define what's feminine. It's ridiculous.

Beyoncé Knowles-Carter (1981–)

Ladies were ladies in those days; they did not do things for themselves.

Gwen Raverat (1885–1957)

Virtue can only flourish amongst equals.

Mary Wollstonecraft Godwin (1759–1797)

MEN

No man is a hero to his valet.

Anne-Marie Bigot de Cornuel (1605–1694)

~~~

Men are luxuries, not necessities.

Cher (1946–)

~~~

Mad, bad, and dangerous to know.

*Lady Caroline Lamb (1785–1828) on
her former lover, Lord Byron*

~~~

. . . as for you men, you may, if you
please, live and be slaves.

*Boudica (c. 30–c. 61 AD), scornfully announcing her
resolve to resist the Romans, to conquer or die*

~~~

I require only three things in a man: he must
be handsome, ruthless and stupid.

Dorothy Parker (1893–1967)

If there is anything disagreeable going on
men are always sure to get out of it . . .

Jane Austen (1775–1817)

I like my men like I like my coffee.
I don't drink coffee.

Ellen DeGeneres (1958–)

Never trust a husband too far,
nor a bachelor too near.

Helen Rowland (1875–1950)

Gout is very much in my line, gentlemen are not.

Elizabeth Garrett Anderson (1836–1917)

There is no greater ninny than
a man who thinks himself cunning,
nor any one wiser than he who
knows he is not so.

*Margaret of Navarre (Marguerite d'Angoulême,
Queen of Navarre, 1492–1549)*

Good morning, gentlemen both.

Queen Elizabeth I (1533–1603) greeting
a group of eighteen tailors

Somehow a bachelor never quite gets over the idea
that he is a thing of beauty and a boy forever.

Helen Rowland (1875–1950)

A man's mind, what there is of it, has always the
advantage of being masculine – as the smallest birch
tree is of a higher kind than the most soaring palm
– and even his ignorance is of a sounder quality.

George Eliot (Mary Ann Evans, 1819–1890)

A self-made man is one who believes in
luck and sends his son to Oxford.

Christina Stead (1902–1983)

In men this blunder still you find
All think their little set mankind.

Hannah More (1745–1833)

The more I see of men, the more I admire dogs.

Marie de Rabutin-Chantal, Madame de Sévigné (1626–1696) (also attributed to Jeanne-Marie, Madame Roland [1754–1793], Madame de Staël [1766–1817], and Ouida [Louise Ramé or de la Ramé, 1839–1908])

Men explain things to me, still. And no man has ever apologized for explaining, wrongly, things that I know and they don't.

Rebecca Solnit (1961–)

There wouldn't be half as much fun in the world if it weren't for children and men, and there ain't a mite of difference between them under the skins.

Ellen Glasgow (1873–1945)

Why we oppose votes for men . . . because men are too emotional to vote. Their conduct at baseball games and political conventions shows this, while their innate tendency to appeal to force renders them particularly unfit for the task of government.

Alice Duer Miller (1874–1942)

The follies which a man regrets most
in his life are those which he didn't commit
when he had the opportunity.

Helen Rowland (1875–1950)

He is every other inch a gentleman.

Rebecca West (1892–1983)

I fear nothing so much as a man
who is witty all day long.

*Marie de Rabutin-Chantal,
Madame de Sévigné (1626–1696)*

The way to a man's heart is through his stomach.

Fanny Fern (Sara Payson Parton, 1811–1872)

Adam's ready acquiescence with his wife's proposal,
does not savor much of that superiority in
strength of mind, which is arrogated by man.

Sarah Moore Grimké (1792–1873)

MEN AND WOMEN

Why are women . . . so much more interesting
to men than men are to women?

Virginia Woolf (1882–1941)

The hardest task in a girl's life is to prove to
a man that his intentions are serious.

Helen Rowland (1875–1950)

Man forgives woman anything save
the wit to outwit him.

Minna Antrim (1861–1950)

The usual masculine disillusionment in
discovering that a woman has a brain.

Margaret Mitchell (1900–1949)

If you want something said, ask a man.
If you want something done, ask a woman.

Margaret Thatcher (1925–2013)

Women have to be twice as good
to get half as far as men.

Agnes MacPhail (1890–1954)

\\\\\\\\\\\

In passing, also, I'd like to say that the first time
Adam had a chance he laid the blame on woman.

Nancy, Lady Astor (1879–1964)

\\\\\\\\\\\

I'm not denyin' the women are foolish: God
Almighty made 'em to match the men.

George Eliot (Mary Ann Evans, 1819–1890)

\\\\\\\\\\\

Love is the whole history of a woman's
life, it is but an episode in a man's.

Germaine Necker, Madame de Staël (1766–1817)

\\\\\\\\\\\

Women must come off the pedestal.
Men put us up there to get us out of the way.

Viscountess Rhondda (1883–1958)

Stupid men, forever prone
To fix the blame on woman's reason,
When 'tis merely your own treason
That creates her fault alone!

Juana Inés de la Cruz (1651–1695)

\\\\\\\\

History tells me nothing that does not either
vex or weary me; the men are all so good for
nothing, and hardly any women at all.

Jane Austen (1775–1817)

\\\\\\\\

It is delightful to be a woman; but every man
thanks the Lord devoutly that he isn't one.

Olive Schreiner (1855–1920)

\\\\\\\\

For just as women's bodies are softer than
men's, so their understanding is sharper.

Christine de Pizan (1364–c. 1430)

I will not say that women are better than men,
but I will say that men are not so wise
as I would wish them to be . . .

*Ester Sowernam (*Ester Hath Hanged Haman, *c. 1617)*

〰〰〰〰

I love men, not because they are men,
but because they are not women.

Christina, Queen of Sweden (1626–1689)

〰〰〰〰

A good woman inspires a man; a brilliant woman
interests him; a beautiful woman fascinates
him; and a sympathetic woman gets him.

Helen Rowland (1875–1950)

〰〰〰〰

. . . when women are the advisers, the lords of creation
don't take the advice till they have persuaded themselves
that it is just what they intended to do; then they act upon
it, and if it succeeds, they give the weaker vessel half the
credit of it; if it fails, they generously give her the whole.

Louisa May Alcott (1832–1888)

A woman despises a man for loving
her unless she returns his love.

Elizabeth Stoddard (1823–1902)

She did observe, with some dismay, that far from
conquering all, love lazily sidestepped practical problems.

Jean Stafford (1915–1979)

I've met Mr Wrong. I've met several Mr
Reasonably Okays. I've spent a very long
afternoon in a bus shelter with Mr Halitosis.

Victoria Wood (1953–2016)

In matters of the heart nothing is
true except the improbable.

Germaine Necker, Madame de Staël (1766–1817)

Tears may be dried up, but the heart – never.

Marguerite de Valois (1553–1615)

We don't believe in rheumatism and true
love until after the first attack.

Marie von Ebner-Eschenbach (1830–1916)

~

love is a very papithatick thing as well
as troublesom and tiresome . . .

Marjory Fleming (1803–1811)

~

Nothing to be done without a bribe
I find, in love as well as law.

Susannah Centlivre (c. 1669–1723)

~

Love never dies of starvation, but often of indigestion.

Ninon (Anne) de Lenclos (1620–1705)

~

Now love the limb-loosener sweeps me away . . .

Sappho (c. 630–c. 570 BC)

Remember my unalterable maxim,
'When we love we always have something to say.'

Lady Mary Wortley Montagu (1689–1762)

We cannot really love anybody with whom we never laugh.

Agnes Repplier (1858–1950)

[Nothing] . . . leads to love. It is love who throws himself across your path. And then he either blocks it for ever or, if he abandons it, leaves it in rack and ruin.

(Sidonie-Gabrielle) Colette (1873–1954)

If only one could tell
true love from false love
as one can tell mushrooms
from toadstools.

Katherine Mansfield (1888–1923)

MATRIMONY

I married beneath me. All women do.

Nancy, Lady Astor (1879–1964)

When a girl marries, she exchanges the attentions
of many men for the inattention of one.

Helen Rowland (1875–1950)

A positive engagement to marry a certain person at
a certain time, at all haps and hazards, I have always
considered the most ridiculous thing on earth.

Jane Welsh Carlyle (1801–1866)

Any intelligent woman who reads the marriage contract,
and then goes into it, deserves all the consequences.

Isadora Duncan (1878–1927)

I've married a few people I shouldn't
have, but haven't we all?

Mamie Van Doren (1931–)

Marriage is the result of the longing for the
deep, deep peace of the double bed after
the hurly-burly of the chaise-longue.

Mrs Patrick Campbell (Beatrice Stella Tanner, 1865–1940)

A husband is what is left of a lover, after
the nerve has been extracted.

Helen Rowland (1875–1950)

Happiness in marriage is entirely a matter of chance.

Jane Austen (1775–1817)

Marriage is a lottery in which men stake their
liberty and women their happiness.

Renée de Chateauneuf-Rieux (1550–1587)

So that ends my first experience with matrimony,
which I always thought a highly overrated performance.

Isadora Duncan (1878–1927)

I've been too fucking busy – or vice versa.

Dorothy Parker (1893–1967) upon being asked by her editor for more stories, whilst on her honeymoon

Girls! Girls! . . . never develop a reputation for being clever. It will put you out of the matrimonial running as effectually as though it had been circulated that you had leprosy.

(Stella Marian Sarah) Miles Franklin (1879–1954)

Single women have a dreadful propensity for being poor – which is one very strong argument in favour of matrimony.

Jane Austen (1775–1817)

When you see what some girls marry, you realize how they must hate to work for a living.

Helen Rowland (1875–1950)

I have very little of Mr Blake's company. He is always in paradise.

Catherine Blake of her husband, William (1757–1827)

That is partly why women marry – to keep up
the fiction of being in the hub of things.

Elizabeth Bowen (1899–1973)

An archaeologist is the best husband any woman can
have: the older she gets, the more interested he is in her.

Agatha Christie (1890–1976)

Marriage, to women as to men, must be a luxury,
not a necessity; an incident of life, not all of it.

Susan Brownell Anthony (1820–1906)

A lady's imagination is very rapid; it jumps from
admiration to love, from love to matrimony in a moment.

Jane Austen (1775–1817)

The people people have for friends
Your common sense appall,
But the people people marry
Are the queerest folk of all.

Charlotte Perkins Gilman (1860–1935)

No divorcees were included, except those who had shown signs of penitence by being remarried to the very wealthy.

Edith Wharton (1862–1937)

In a successful marriage there is no such thing as one's way. There is only the way of both, only the bumpy, dusty, difficult, but always mutual path!

Phyllis McGinley (1905–1978)

Marriage is the grave or tomb of wit.

Margaret Cavendish, Duchess of Newcastle (1617–1673)

A woman, let her be as good as she may, has got to put up with the life her husband makes for her.

George Eliot (Mary Ann Evans, 1819–1890)

It is always incomprehensible to a man that a woman should ever refuse an offer of marriage.

Jane Austen (1775–1817); she herself refused offers of marriage, and on one occasion, having actually accepted, changed her mind the following morning

. . . my husbands have been very unlucky.

Lucrezia Borgia (1480–1519), after the
murder of her second husband

Indeed he has all the qualities that would make
a husband tolerable – battlement, veranda,
stable, etc., no grins and no glass in his eye.

George Eliot (Mary Ann Evans, 1819–1890)

It is a truth universally acknowledged,
that a single man in possession of a good
fortune, must be in want of a wife.

Jane Austen (1775–1817)

Ask half the married women in the
nation how they became wives: they will
tell you their friends urged them.

Fanny Burney (Frances, Madame d'Arblay, 1752–1840)

A real marriage bears no resemblance
to these marriages of interest or ambition.
It is two lovers who live together.

Lady Mary Wortley Montagu (1689–1762)

Now at least I know where he is.

*Queen Alexandra (1844–1925) after the
death of her husband, Edward VII*

Having once embarked on your marital voyage,
it is impossible not to be aware that you make no
way and that the sea is not within sight – that,
in fact, you are exploring an enclosed basin.

George Eliot (Mary Ann Evans, 1819–1890)

Marriage: a souvenir of love.

Helen Rowland (1875–1950)

The state of matrimony is
a dangerous disease: far better
to take drink in my opinion.

Marie de Rabutin-Chantal,
Madame de Sévigné (1626–1696)

My own, or other people's?

Peggy Guggenheim (1898–1975), in answer to the question 'How many husbands have you had?'

I would rather be a beggar and single, than a Queen and married . . . I should call the wedding ring the yoke ring.

Queen Elizabeth I (1533–1603)

. . . a state that causes the misery of three quarters of the human race.

Françoise d'Aubigné, Madame de Maintenon (1635–1719)

Dear, never forget one little point: it's my business, you just work here.

Elizabeth Arden (1878–1966) to her husband, manager of her company

FRIENDS
AND
ENEMIES

I always felt that the great high privilege,
relief and comfort of friendship was
that one had to explain nothing.

Katherine Mansfield (1888–1923)

'Stay' is a charming word in a friend's vocabulary.

Louisa May Alcott (1832–1888)

The heart may think it knows better:
the senses know that absence blots people
out. We have really no absent friends.

Elizabeth Bowen (1899–1973)

Animals are such agreeable friends – they ask
no questions, they pass no criticisms.

George Eliot (Mary Ann Evans, 1819–1890)

Friends can see defects with the naked eye, however weak that organ may be; but too frequently require magnifying glasses to discover good qualities.

Marguerite, Lady Blessington (1789–1849)

Every murderer is probably somebody's old friend.

Agatha Christie (1890–1976)

Life becomes useless and insipid when we have no longer either friends or enemies.

Christina, Queen of Sweden (1626–1689)

Intimacies between women often go backwards, beginning in revelations and ending up in small talk, without loss of esteem.

Elizabeth Bowen (1899–1973)

I have lost friends, some by
death . . . others through sheer
inability to cross the street.

Virginia Woolf (1882–1941)

People wish their enemies dead – but I do not;
I say give them the gout, give them the stone!

Lady Mary Wortley Montagu (1689–1762)

There are times when one cannot lift a blade of
grass without finding a serpent underneath it.

Marceline Desbordes-Valmore (1786–1859)

Yes'm, old friends is always best, 'less you can catch
a new one that's fit to make an old one out of.

Sarah Orne Jewett (1849–1909)

True friendship is never serene.

Marie de Rabutin-Chantal, Madame de Sévigné (1626–1696)

Treat your friends as you do your pictures,
and place them in their best light.

Lady Randolph Churchill (née Jennie Jerome, 1854–1921)

Business, you know, may bring money,
but friendship hardly ever does.

Jane Austen (1775–1817)

My true friends have always given me that supreme proof
of devotion, a spontaneous aversion to the man I loved.

(Sidonie-Gabrielle) Colette (1873–1954)

Friendships begin with liking or gratitude
– roots that can be pulled up.

George Eliot (Mary Ann Evans, 1819–1890)

To have a good enemy, choose a friend;
he knows where to strike.

Diane de Poitiers (1499–1566)

God gave us our relatives; thank God
we can choose our friends.

Ethel Watts Mumford (1878–1940)

FAMILY

For it is impossible for a man to put forward fair
and honest views about our affairs if he has not, like
everyone else, children whose lives may be at stake.

Aspasia (c. 470–c. 400 BC),
speech written for Pericles

The best way to keep children home is to make the home
atmosphere pleasant and let the air out of the tires.

Dorothy Parker (1893–1967)

. . . for the sins of children rise up
in judgement against their parents.

Lady Caroline Lamb (1785–1828)

I never met anyone who didn't have a very
smart child. What happens to these children,
you wonder, when they reach adulthood?

Fran Lebowitz (1950–)

The family – that dear octopus from whose
tentacles we never quite escape.

Dodie Smith (1896–1990)

It is not a bad thing that children should occasionally, and politely, put parents in their place.

(Sidonie-Gabrielle) Colette (1873–1954)

Most mothers think that to keep young people away from love-making it is enough never to speak of it in their presence.

Marie-Madeleine, Madame de La Fayette (1634–1693)

Politeness, that cementer of friendship and soother of enmities, is nowhere so much required, and so frequently outraged, as in family circles.

Marguerite, Lady Blessington (1789–1849)

. . . children servants master father mother, things that though they are blessings yet often they prove otherwise, and the best of them have days in which one thinks one could live without them.

Margaret Godolphin (1652–1678)

Childhood is never troubled with foresight.

Fanny Burney (Frances, Madame d'Arblay, 1752–1840)

My father warned me about men and booze, but he never mentioned a word about women and cocaine.

Tallulah Bankhead (1902–1968)

THE SELF

I know they are most deceived that
trusteth most in themselves.

Queen Elizabeth I (1533–1603)

You grow up the day you have your
first real laugh at yourself.

Ethel Barrymore (1879–1959)

I have often wished I had time to cultivate modesty
. . . but I am too busy thinking about myself.

Edith Sitwell (1887–1964)

Don't be so humble – you are not that great.

Golda Meir (1898–1978)

. . . I'm not going to lie down
and let trouble walk over me.

Ellen Glasgow (1873–1945)

There are some secrets which scarcely admit of being disclosed even to ourselves.

Jane West (1758–1852)

My vigour, vitality and cheek repel me. I am the kind of woman I would run away from.

Nancy, Lady Astor (1879–1964)

Whenever anyone has called me a bitch, I have taken it as a compliment. To me, a bitch is assertive, unapologetic, demanding, intimidating, intelligent, fiercely protective, in control – all very positive attributes.

Margaret Cho (1968–)

I am never afraid of what I know.

Anna Sewell (1820–1878)

For whomsoever I do good they harm me most.

Sappho (c. 630–c. 570 BC)

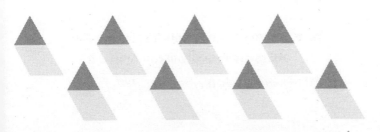

I think it's good for a person to spend time alone. It gives them an opportunity to discover who they are and to figure out why they are always alone.

Amy Sedaris (1961–)

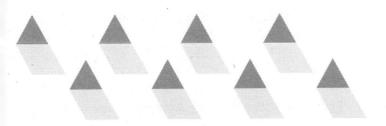

How prone we are to blame others, when
we ourselves only are in fault.

Marguerite, Lady Blessington (1789–1849)

The Jews have produced only three originative
geniuses: Christ, Spinoza, and myself.

Gertrude Stein (1874–1946)

Real education should educate us out of self
into something far finer; into a selflessness
which links us with all humanity.

Nancy, Lady Astor (1879–1964)

I am not at all the sort of person you and I took me for.

Jane Welsh Carlyle (1801–1866)

'Know thyself' is a most superfluous direction. We can't
avoid it. We can only hope that no one else knows.

Ivy Compton-Burnett (1884–1969)

To have the courage of your excess –
to find the limit of yourself.

Katherine Mansfield (1888–1923)

I don't like to gamble, but if there's one
thing I'm willing to bet on, it's myself.

Beyoncé Knowles-Carter (1981–)

I can see that the Lady has a genius for ruling,
whilst I have a genius for not being ruled.

Jane Welsh Carlyle (1801–1866)

I give myself sometimes admirable advice,
but am incapable of taking it.

Lady Mary Wortley Montagu (1689–1762)

. . . everything seems insupportable to me. This may
very well be because I am insupportable myself.

Marie-Anne, Marquise du Deffand (1697–1780)

I am one of the people who love the why of things.

Catherine the Great, Empress of Russia (1729–1796)

Find out who you are and do it on purpose.

Dolly Parton (1946–)

Whenever I dwell for any length of time on my own shortcomings, they gradually begin to seem mild, harmless, rather engaging little things, not at all like the staring defects in other people's characters.

Margaret Halsey (1910–1997)

It is never too late to be what you might have been.

George Eliot (Mary Ann Evans, 1819–1890)

HUMAN
NATURE

Well, of course, people are only human . . .
But it does not seem much for them to be.

Ivy Compton-Burnett (1884–1969)

If only we'd stop trying to be happy, we
could have a pretty good time.

Edith Wharton (1862–1937)

We are far more united and have
far more in common with each other
than things that divide us.

Jo Cox (1974–2016)

We are so vain that we even care for the
opinion of those we don't care for.

Marie von Ebner Eschenbach (1830–1916)

**Curious things, habits.
People themselves never
knew they had them.**

Agatha Christie (1890–1976)

People are always willing to follow advice
when it accords with their own wishes . . .

Marguerite, Lady Blessington (1789–1849)

It is vain to say human beings ought to be satisfied
with tranquillity: they must have action; and
they will make it if they cannot find it.

George Eliot (Mary Ann Evans, 1819–1890)

You know how they say that religion is the opiate
of the masses? Well, I took masses of opiates religiously.

Carrie Fisher (1956–2016)

Science may have found a cure for most evils;
but it has found no remedy for the worst of
them all – the apathy of human beings.

Helen Keller (1880–1968)

There are only two distinct classes
of people on this earth: those who espouse
enthusiasm and those who despise it.

Germaine Necker, Madame de Staël (1766–1817)

Some people are moulded by their
admirations, others by their hostilities.

Elizabeth Bowen (1899–1973)

The cynic says 'blessed is he who expecteth nothing for
he shall not be disappointed.' I say 'blessed is he who
expecteth everything, for he can't always be disappointed.'

Tallulah Bankhead (1902–1968)

It is natural to avoid those to whom we have
been too much obliged . . . uncommon generosity
causes neglect rather than ingratitude.

Héloïse (c. 1098–1164)

They say revenge is a dish best eaten cold,
but for most people, by the time it's ready to
eat, they just don't fancy it anymore.

Jo Brand (1957–)

Someone has somewhere commented on the fact that
millions long for immortality who don't know what
to do with themselves on a rainy Sunday afternoon.

Susan Ertz (1894–1985)

I enjoy vast delight in the folly of mankind;
and, God be praised, that is an inexhaustible
source of entertainment.

Lady Mary Wortley Montagu (1689–1762)

'Tis easy enough to be pleasant
When life flows along like a song;
But the man worth while is the one who will smile
When everything goes dead wrong.

Ella Wheeler Wilcox (1855–1919)

. . . people who do not get into scrapes are a great deal less interesting than those who do.

Murasaki Shikibu (c. 973–c. 1031)

One half of the world cannot understand the pleasures of the other.

Jane Austen (1775–1817)

The human heart has hidden treasures, In secret held, in silence sealed.

Charlotte Brontë (1816–1855)

WISDOM
AND
LEARNING

The human mind always makes progress,
but it is a progress in spirals.

Germaine Necker, Madame de Staël (1766–1817)

Genius is the gold in the mine; talent is the
miner that works and brings it out.

Marguerite, Lady Blessington (1789–1849)

It takes a lot of time to be a genius, you have to sit
around so much doing nothing, really doing nothing.

Gertrude Stein (1874–1946)

No one can arrive from being talented alone. God
gives talent, work transforms talent into genius.

Anna Pavlova (1881–1931)

Follow your passion. Stay true to yourself. Never
follow someone else's path unless you're in
the woods and you're lost and you see a path.
By all means, you should follow that.

Ellen DeGeneres (1958–)

Genius, whether locked up in a cell
or roaming at large, is always solitary.

*George Sand (Amandine-Aurore Lucille Dupin,
Baronne Dudevant, 1804–1876)*

The majority of minds are no more to
be controlled by strong reason than plum-
pudding is to be grasped by sharp pincers.

George Eliot (Mary Ann Evans, 1819–1890)

I read Shakespeare and the Bible, and I can shoot
dice. That's what I call a liberal education.

Tallulah Bankhead (1902–1968)

True knowledge consists in knowing things not words.

Lady Mary Wortley Montagu (1689–1762)

It is not depravity that afflicts the human race
so much as a general lack of intelligence.

Agnes Repplier (1858–1950)

Listen, everyone is entitled to my opinion.

Madonna (1958–)

Since when was genius found respectable?

Elizabeth Barrett Browning (1806–1861)

Science may carry us to Mars, but it will leave
the earth peopled as ever by the inept.

Agnes Repplier (1858–1950)

It takes people a long time to learn the
difference between talent and genius, especially
ambitious young men and women.

Louisa May Alcott (1832–1888)

Brass shines as fair to the ignorant as gold to the goldsmith.

Queen Elizabeth I (1533–1603)

Better build schoolrooms for the boy,
Than cells and gibbets for the man.

Eliza Cook (1818–1889)

Teach him to think for himself? Oh, my God, teach him rather to think like other people!

Mary Shelley (1797–1851) on her son's education

Yet if thou didst but know how little wit governs this mighty universe.

Aphra Behn (1640–1689)

People are never so near playing the fool as when they think themselves wise.

Lady Mary Wortley Montagu (1689–1762)

All our talents increase in the using, and every faculty, both good and bad, strengthens by exercise.

Anne Brontë (1820–1849)

Too much rigidity on the part of teachers should be followed by a brisk spirit of insubordination on the part of the taught.

Agnes Repplier (1858–1950)

Prejudices, it is well known, are most difficult to eradicate from the heart whose soil has never been loosened or fertilized by education; they grow there, firm as weeds among rocks.

Charlotte Brontë (1816–1855)

LIFE

Life is either always a tightrope
or a feather bed. Give me the tightrope.

Edith Wharton (1862–1937)

It is not true that life is one damn thing after
another – it's one damn thing over and over.

Edna St Vincent Millay (1892–1950)

If my life wasn't funny it would just be
true, and that is unacceptable.

Carrie Fisher (1956–2016)

Life appears to me too short to be spent in
nursing animosity or registering wrong.

Charlotte Brontë (1816–1855)

What I love about noise is that it camouflages life.

Germaine Necker, Madame de Staël (1766–1817)

It never occurred to me to be happy with my lot.

Jessica Mitford (1917–1996)

Sooner or later we all discover that the important moments in life are not the advertised ones, not the birthdays, the graduations, the weddings, not the great goals achieved. The real milestones are less prepossessing. They come to the door of memory unannounced, stray dogs that amble in, sniff round a bit, and simply never leave. Our lives are measured by these.

Susan Brownell Anthony (1820–1906)

I have learned to live each day as it comes, and not to borrow trouble by dreading tomorrow. It is the dark menace of the future that makes cowards of us all.

Dorothy Dix (1870–1951)

The surest way to get a thing in this life is to be prepared for doing without it, to the exclusion even of hope.

Jane Welsh Carlyle (1801–1866)

I'll quit coffee. It won't be easy drinking my
Baileys straight, but I'll get used to it. It'll
still be the best part of waking up.

Megan Mullally (1958–)

As soon as life becomes bearable we stop analysing
it . . . A tranquil day is spoiled by being examined.

*George Sand (Amandine-Aurore Lucille Dupin,
Baronne Dudevant, 1804–1876)*

Courage is the price that life exacts for granting peace.

Amelia Earhart (1898–1937)

Instant gratification takes too long.

Carrie Fisher (1956–2016)

Life is so constructed, that the event does not,
cannot, will not match the expectation.

Charlotte Brontë (1816–1855)

Nothing in life is to be feared.
It is only to be understood.

Marie Curie (1867–1934)

If I had to live my life again, I'd make
the same mistakes, only sooner.

Tallulah Bankhead (1902–1968)

I slept, and dreamed that life was beauty
I woke – and found that life was duty.

Ellen Sturgis Hooper (1816–1841)

I hate housework! You make the beds, you do the dishes
– and six months later you have to start all over again.

Joan Rivers (1933–2014)

Life was meant to be lived, and curiosity must
be kept alive. One must never, for whatever
reason, turn his back on life.

Eleanor Roosevelt (1884–1962)

**To live is so startling
it leaves little time for
anything else.**

Emily Dickinson (1830–1886)

PHILOSOPHY

No idea is so antiquated that it was not
once modern. No idea is so modern that
it will not some day be antiquated.

Ellen Glasgow (1873–1945)

My definition is of a man up in a balloon,
with his family and friends holding the ropes
which confine him to the earth and
trying to haul him down.

Louisa May Alcott (1832–1888)
on how she sees a philosopher

One way of getting an idea of our fellow countrymen's
miseries is to go and look at their pleasures.

George Eliot (Mary Ann Evans, 1819–1890)

He who influences the thought of his times,
influences all the times that follow. He
has made his impress on eternity.

Hypatia (c. 360–415 AD)

No philosophy, my son:
it is of no use to an emperor.

Agrippina the Younger (15–59 AD), advice to Nero

A fool bolts pleasure, then complains
of moral indigestion.

Minna Antrim (1861–1950)

Loneliness is solitude with a problem.

Maggie Nelson (1973–)

Nothing is so good as it seems beforehand.

George Eliot (Mary Ann Evans, 1819–1890)

A vacuum can only exist, I imagine,
by the things that enclose it.

Zelda Fitzgerald (1900–1948)

There is always a 'but' in this imperfect world.

Anne Brontë (1820–1849)

There 〰️

It behoved that there should be sin; but all shall be well,
and all shall be well, and all manner of thing shall be well.

Julian of Norwich (c. 1342–c. 1430)

There 〰️

When one door of happiness closes, another opens;
but often we look so long at the closed door that we
do not see the one which has been opened for us.

Helen Keller (1880–1968)

There 〰️

We realize the importance of our voices
only when we are silenced.

Malala Yousafzai (1997–)

There 〰️

They who see only what they wish to see in
those around them are very fortunate.

Marie Bashkirtseff (1860–1884)

We cannot take anything for granted,
beyond the first mathematical formula.
Question everything else.

Maria Mitchell (1818–1889)

All sins are attempts to fill voids.

Simone Weil (1909–1943)

There are two ways of spreading light:
to be the candle, or the mirror that reflects it.

Edith Wharton (1862–1937)

No man chooses evil because it is evil; he only
mistakes it for happiness, the good he seeks.

Mary Wollstonecraft Godwin (1759–1797)

No good deed
goes unpunished.

Clare Boothe Luce (1903–1987)

Experience is a good teacher,
but she sends in terrific bills.

Minna Antrim (1861–1950)

I avoid looking forward or backward,
and try to keep looking upward.

Charlotte Brontë (1816–1855)

Considering how dangerous everything
is nothing is frightening.

Gertrude Stein (1874–1946)

So this gentleman said a girl with brains ought
to do something with them besides think.

Anita Loos (1893–1981)

Saddle your dreams afore you ride 'em.

Mary Webb (1881–1927)

I make the most of all that comes,
and the least of all that goes.

Sara Teasdale (1884–1933)

Why not seize the pleasure at once?
How often is happiness destroyed by
preparation, foolish preparation!

Jane Austen (1775–1817)

Time, that omnipotent effacer of eternal passions . . .

Marguerite, Lady Blessington (1789–1849)

It is sometimes best to slide over thoughts
and not go to the bottom of them.

*Marie de Rabutin-Chantal,
Madame de Sévigné (1626–1696)*

Avoiding danger is no safer in the long run than outright exposure. The fearful are caught as often as the bold.

Helen Keller (1880–1968)

When one has been threatened with a great injustice, one accepts a smaller as a favour.

Jane Welsh Carlyle (1801–1866)

The beauty of the world, which is so soon to perish, has two edges, one of laughter, one of anguish, cutting the heart asunder.

Virginia Woolf (1882–1941)

DEATH AND LAST WORDS

While we are young the idea of death
or failure is intolerable to us; even the
possibility of ridicule we cannot bear.

Isak Dinesen (Karen Blixen, 1885–1962)

I have a horror of death; the dead are so soon forgotten.
But when I die, they'll have to remember me.

Emily Dickinson (1830–1886)

I tell my younger friends that no matter how
I go, I wanted it reported that I drowned in
moonlight, strangled by my own bra.

Carrie Fisher (1956–2016)

There's something dreadfully
decisive about a beheading.

Agnes Smedley (1892–1950)

My dear – the people we should
have been seen dead with.

*Rebecca West (1892–1983), telegram to
Noël Coward on learning that they had
both been in the Nazi 'Black Book'*

Death and taxes and childbirth! There's never
any convenient time for any of them.

Margaret Mitchell (1900–1949)

We met . . . Dr Hall in such very deep mourning that
either his mother, his wife or himself must be dead.

Jane Austen (1775–1817)

Matter and death are mortal illusions.

*Mary Baker Eddy (1821–1910), herself
now presumably a mortal illusion*

I think we could jam a bit more
in our coffins than we do. I'm going
to have some books, some I haven't
finished or haven't read, some
feathers and nice bits and pieces,
the odd note. Just on the journey
for the next bit.

Joanna Lumley (1946–)

If you will send for a doctor I will see him now.

Emily Brontë (1818–1848)

Of course I'm against it.

*Jessica Mitford (1917–1996) responding
to Evelyn Waugh's review of her book,* The
American Way of Death, *in which he said she did
not have 'a plainly stated attitude to death'*

Monsieur, I beg your pardon.
I did not do it on purpose.

*Marie-Antoinette, Queen Consort
of France (1755–1793), as she stumbled over the
executioner's foot on the way to the guillotine*

Let me go! Let me go!

Clara Barton (1821–1912)

Take courage, Charlotte, take courage!

Anne Brontë (1820–1849)

Beautiful.

Elizabeth Barrett Browning (1806–1861),
when asked how she was feeling

How imperious one is when one
no longer has the time to be polite.

Jeanne-Louise-Henriette Campan (1752–1822),
who had just issued an order to a servant

I want to go and go, and then drop dead in the
middle of something I'm loving to do. And if
that doesn't happen, if I wind up sitting in a
wheelchair, at least I'll have my high heels on.

Dolly Parton (1946–)

Ah, my God, I am dead!

*Catherine de Médicis, Queen Consort of France
(1519–1589), slightly anticipating events*

Nothing but death.

*Jane Austen (1775–1817),
when asked what she required*

What is the answer? [No reply. Laughs]
In that case what is the question?

Gertrude Stein (1874–1946)

I'm going to Dr Caldwell's for one
of my regular treatments.

Jeanne Eagels (1890–1929)

Oh that peace may come. Bertie!

*Queen Victoria (1819–1901), who had been
waiting to see her beloved Albert*

Yes, it is indeed frightful weather for
a journey as long as the one before me.

Marie-Thérèse of Austria,
Queen Consort of France (1638–1683)

Today I am better, but if you wish for another cheerful
evening with your old friend, there is no time to be lost.

Mary Russell Mitford (1787–1855)

I see no reason why the existence of Harriet
Martineau should be perpetuated.

Harriet Martineau (1802–1876)

They have made me tipsy. Stocky! Stocky!

Charlotte Augusta, Princess of Wales (1796–1817),
calling for Baron Stockmar, the court
physician (she died in childbirth)

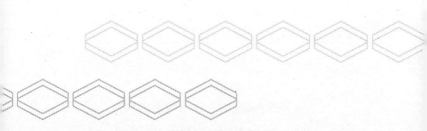

Go first. At least I can spare you the pain of seeing my blood flow.

Jeanne-Marie, Madame Roland (1754–1793),
herself a revolutionary, to a frightened old man,
both about to be guillotined by the Jacobins

Get my Swan costume ready.

Anna Pavlova (1881–1931)

That will be nice.

Mary Webb (1881–1927), told that everyone would gather for tea that afternoon

It has all been very interesting.

Lady Mary Wortley Montagu (1689–1762)

Is it not meningitis?

Louisa May Alcott (1832–1888)

Except taxes.

Elisa Bonaparte (1777–1820), sister of Napoleon, concluding the remark 'Nothing is as certain as death . . .'